LIFE, DEATH, AND LIVING WITH A DEATH WISH

POET, MADMAN, MYSTIC

AUTOBIOGRAPHY OF A POET IN POETRY

BOOK III

THE PHOENIX TRILOGY

Daylight Publishing
With Lulu Publishing

Roy. E. Day Jr.

Edited and Cover by Helen Manget

Dedication

To my parents, especially thank to my father for his financial support of this project, siblings and their children, my friends, cousins, spiritual teachers and to this beautiful planet, our Mother Earth.

Introduction

This three book autobiography in poetry covers the first forty years of my life, with the poetry starting at seventeen. I have attempted to make it primarily poetry, but have supplied enough prose to provide context for the interested. It was collected and first edited in 1994 and although published years later the original time frame, attitude, and perspective was retained.

TABLE OF CONTENTS

Life, Death, and Living with a Death Wish 1
    Waves of Life 7
    Loser's Lament 9
    Drank Myself to Sleep this Morning 10
    Self-Searching 12
    Too Many Scars 13
    Scared of the Silence 14
    The Fight Went On 14
    Dry Heaves 15
    Hopes of the Fallen 17
    Images of My Dreams 19
    American Bar Scene 20
    Oblivion Disease 23
    Easter Morning 24
    The Night Calls My Soul 25
    Going Into the Night 26
    The Hours After Midnight 27
    Life and Death 29
    Spiritual Warrior's Life-code 29
    Cycles of Desperation 30
    Picking Up the Pieces 31
    Soul Dispossessed 32
    Recklessness 34
    Tortured Sleep of the Damned 35
    Touch of Time 36
    Rend A Tear 37
    Light In Darkness 40
    I Woke Up Screaming 40
    Anything 41
    From Heart to Hand 42
    Hope 44
    World Gone Mad 45
    Play With Death 45
    Still Living When 46
    Suicide's A Waste 47
    Your Choices 48
    Tired of the Waste 49
    Hold on to Strength 50
    I Believe 50
    Kiss the Sky 51

Modern Urban Landscape 53
No Sympathy for Some Suicides 54
Love the Night 55
Howl in the Moonlight 55
Guns and Hormones 57
When 58
The Golden Green 58
Why 59
After A Carwreck 61
Death Wish 63
Moderation and Extremes 64
Crosses and Abuses 65
Indian Soul 66
Hot Eyes, Cold Blue Steel 67
Come and Share My Sickness 70
Dark Corners of Her Soul 74
Mellow Fellow 76
What Fine Webs 76
Savagery of Love - the Lust for Justice 77
Ode to the Outlaws 78
Rebel Bred 80
Prey or Predator 81
Urges Aren't Frantic 82

Political, Historical, and Social Commentary 83
American 83
Perfect Piece 85
Progress 87
Home 88
Choice 90
1982 Surprise 91
Change 92
Que San 93
Long Tine Gone 94
Rocked the World 95
A Thousand Points of Light 96
In the Ricefields 97
Viet Nam Remembered 99
Like They Should Have 100
Spring Coming 101
The Murder Of Innocence 102
Early 70's - Status Test/Acid Test 103

Viet Nam and Now - Stand Tall for Freedom	104
Advice to the Streets	107
1991 - So Far, So Good	110
Crack is Evil	111
God In Man	112
Serve Each Other	113
Antietam Creek	113
1992 - God Bless Bill Clinton	114
America the Free	115
Alas Columbia	115
Blue Berets	116
Tired of the Gripers	117
Nostradamus	119
Cleaning House	120
Thirty Thousand Murders by Sixteen	121
Atlanta's Uglification	122
Trees of My Childhood	123
Concrete America	125

Earthsongs/Goddessongs ... 127

Earth Reborn	127
Her Love Transcends	128
Summer Symphony	129
Call of the Heat	130
Natural Meditation	131
Miss the Caribbean	132
Brother Crow	133
Winter Cleansing	134
Hear the Song of Life	135
Learn More From Nature	137
Prefer the Reservation	138
In Love With the Earth	139
Earthsongs	140
Must be Stopped	142
Walk With Beauty	142
Used to Be	143
Snow	144
Hate the Destroyers	144
Natural Connection	145
Care for Our Mother	146
Advice to the Builder from Mother Earth	147
Dawn Songbirds	148

    Death of the Beauty 149
    A Prayer for Light 150
    Born Of Woman 151

Religious, Mystical, and Occult 152
    Plastic Jesus 153
    An Apology to Jesus 153
    Spiritual Longing 158
    Second Ring of Night 159
    Ode to Isis 160
    A Spirit Goes Shining 161
    A Tribute to Evelyn Eaton 161
    Fabric and Friction of Reality 162
    There is a Good Side to the Darkness 163
    Eternity Waits 164
    Materialists Denial 164
    Tools.. 165
    Invocation of the Sun 166
    Face of God 167
    Prayer to the Gracious Goddess 167
    Ancestors 168
    All Known 169
    Wrestling Devils 170
    Womb of the Worlds 171
    God is a Whale 172
    Insanity, the Lure of Death, and the Dance of Life 172
    Alice Named Isis 175
    God the Goddess - Out of Reach... 176
    Don't Be Waylaid 177
    Excuses.. 178
    The Universe 179
    For God 180
    Need for Forgiveness 180
    Yahweh's Consort 181
    No Longer on Bended Knee 182
    Religion/Liberation - Real Religious Experience......................... 183
    The Miracle of Unanswered Prayer 184
    Catastrophe and the Search for Meaning 185
    That Sacred Somehow-Other... 186
    Iki-ryo 187
    My Revelation 188

Life, Death, and Living with a Death Wish

In <u>Crucifixion and Resurrection, the Rhythms of Life</u> I traced my youth in poetry, went through my accident and rehabilitation, and explained my spiritual searching and the answers I found. It went through my experiences as a nightclub owner, finding and losing love, going through a down and deep-dark period, and my eventual return to college and getting on with my life.

The primary statement of the book is that all Life is lived out in rhythms, day and night, winter - spring - summer - fall, and personally and spiritually, in crucifixions and resurrections. Whether your primary symbols are the Indian's circle, the Christian's cross, a wheel with eight spokes, a six or five pointed star, whatever, everyone experiences highs and lows, experiences the swing of Life's pendulum. I would like to believe that my life's path could be described as a pendulum fixed on an ascending spiral, spiritually evolving upwards towards divinity.

Hopefully all of our paths are like pendulums spiraling upwards towards the divine and we learn and benefit from our lows as well as highs. Often we learn more and are more deeply inspired during our periods of darkness and personal crucifixions than during our best, happiest, or most content times.

Book two, <u>Love, Pleasure, and Pain: The Anatomy of Adultery</u> was simply a love story told in poetry. It involved two women, both of whom I lost, one in possibly tragic circumstances.

This third book overlaps some of the same time as the other two, beginning with my failed business and relationship in Athens, my return to Atlanta, returning to college to study symbolic anthropology, and dealing with alcohol and cocaine abuse. The beginning of this book reflects one of the darkest periods of my life, a time of personal failure. I hadn't succeeded economically; I hadn't lived up to my own standards of behavior or the teachings of my spiritual teachers. There were times during this period that I disliked, even hated myself. Many people in our society have businesses fail or relationships that fall apart. Alcohol and drug abuse are rampant today. People who have gone through these experiences may identify with much in the beginning of this book.

In 1984 I went back out West and returned to the sweat lodge I had attended from 1976 to 1979. It helped to reinvigorate my spiritual life. In 1986 I wrote my honor's thesis, <u>The Shaman Between Worlds</u>. It was at this point that my thesis committee chairwoman suggested that I put my academic pursuits on hold and pursue a literary career. She said that was where my true talent lay and I should follow the path of my talent.

Since then I've worked on several projects, among them a spy novel which involved some characters written as true-believers in Nostradamus. When the Gulf War broke out I switched over to writing a straight commentary on the Nostradamus prophecies, <u>The Nostradamus Scenario</u>, published by Northwest Publishing, due out the summer of '96. I compiled these three books of poetry and am currently working on an occult fiction-detective story.

During the time period of this third book there were women, Debbie, Caitlin, Rhonda, Renee, there were good times and bad, periods of darkness and light. There were long productive periods of self-discipline and there were lapses of self-destruction.

At the present point in my life I have pursued a profession as an author/poet/teacher/sculptor. I now abstain from cocaine or any hard drugs and drink moderately if at all. The medical profession came up with a new generation of nerve pain drugs which has made my life and many thousands more much more pleasant. I still practice the Métis Shamanism Eve taught me and occasionally teach it.

The poems in this book are arranged by their subject matter in a loosely chronological order. A few comments precede each category and are included when necessary. The first subject, which furnishes the title for this work, is that of Thanatos, the classical Greek personification of Death, symbolizing an unconscious lust for death, the death wish, with which I include patterns of self-destruction, including dangerous escapism. These poems also deal with a related subject, the inherent dichotomy of the human personality. We human beings all do contrary things, we are both productive and self-destructive, sometimes rational, sometimes irrational.

My younger brother once satirized me as a person with two basic characteristics. He would pass his hand over his face, show a benevolent face and say "Jesus Christ", then he would pass his hand back over his face again, show a malevolent face and say "Charles Manson". He repeated this several times until the whole table was laughing. Of course, he was exaggerating, but we are all paradoxical, contrary creatures.

It works both ways, sometimes we do the "right thing" when it's not the easiest, or what we childishly want to do, or even best for us. Likewise, sometimes we do the wrong thing, immoral thing, or self-destructive thing that we know in our conscious mind we should not do, yet we follow an inner compulsion to do anyway. Thus a person such as myself, trained as a Métis shaman, a mystic by nature, a poet with some sensitivity can be perceived periodically as a crazed madman with a colossal death wish. There is no doubt in my mind or in those who know me that the mystical and spiritual aspect of my personality, while genuine and sincere, is certainly balanced by a dark, violent, destructive, self-destructive aspect. If I had grown up in Japan I would have thought myself the possessor of an Iki-ryo, a death demon of great destructive power. In the west we think of things differently, and people like me get lectured every so often by the people who love us, and they use the phrase death wish.

The term death wish is not one I have ever ascribed to myself but rather something I have heard from friends and family throughout my life. I would express it differently, saying I seem to experience cyclical needs for excitement, or that every so often my personal demons rise up within me and I feel the need to push the edge, to take risks. The result of which has been a wide variety of scars from a wide variety of activities, some of which I just can't talk about. I've broken major bones five times, had more than six major concussions, I've had guns in my face, I've gone through the windshields of cars, taken out telephone poles, had numerous run-ins with the police, fallen off horses, buildings, and came within nine inches of falling off 14,000 ft. Tioga Pass. I've had more car wrecks than I can remember, but always alone. My dance with death is a solo dance. They use to say I was a cat with nine lives, but I've had way more than nine close calls with death. I quit counting over a decade ago after the thirteenth or fourteenth near-miss.

We all have our inner angels and demons. In expressing myself about how I came to deal with both the spiritual and carnal, benevolent and violent, self-nurturing and self-destructive aspects of the human psyche, I do not want to be misunderstood. All of us human beings live with our dichotomies. I do not mean to glorify stupid risk-taking or self-destructive behavior. I'm certainly not the only human dealing with both the angelic and demonic aspects of the human soul. There is no glory in scars, broken bones, and shame, and I don't mean to glamorize or defend dangerous or self-destructive behavior. If anything, these poems are my attempts to understand such behavior, and describe the struggle to rise above it. If I have exhibited death wish behavior as I've heard my whole life, those same people would tell you it is always balanced by my joyful embrace of Life itself. <u>I love being alive</u> on this little blue-green planet and love the myriad experiences available to us. That being said, these poems do reflect my own and other peoples' love of life as well as flirtations with Thanatos. They begin with a very dark period, but there is always Darkness before the Light.

Waves of Life

All my friends are having children

settled down with jobs and homes

still I find myself a loner

no wife, no kids, no chains of love

All my friends envy me my freedom

they remember younger days of fun

when no one depended on their income

when no one complained or bitched at all

All my friends don't really party

not like those wild, wild days of youth

they're tired from work and raising children

all they really want is rest

And as my friends are having children

my parents age before my eyes

I'd like to have them around forever

I cherish them more as time goes by

And so my friends are having children

with spouses and jobs and kids and homes

and all these years I'm still rebelling

I seek a path that is my own

And so the children now bear children

another wave in the ocean of Life

the new generation spawned by the old

the ebbing, flowing of the tide.

Loser's Lament

I've got the shakes again this morning

it must be seven days

Since I woke up cold stone sober

or gave a damn about the race

I keep on living in this rage now

its silent and its cold

I can't believe that she would leave me

I can't believe I'm all alone

But the fact is that she left me

because of me and nothing else

I don't want to take the credit

but it won't fall on no one else

But more than fickle women

more than self-destruct love

I'm not really being me now

I'm just a shell of my old hopes

I was going to help the world once

I was going to make a change

somehow life on earth seems different

now survival is the game

But I'll keep on keeping on

I don't really have much choice

but I hope I find my way back

to take communion with my soul.

Drank Myself to Sleep this Morning

Drank myself to sleep this morning

the way I sometimes do

When I woke up there were storm clouds

late in the afternoon

I thought about the things she'd said

not long ago, but still the truth

when she told me that the thrill was gone

it was my time for the blues

Time might fade, but it won't change

the wrong I know I did

and whatever the Future hides today

things will never be the same

But I woke up here in Georgia

safe and warm where I belong

this drinking life may kill me

but at least they'll bury me at home.

Self-Searching

Sometimes the bad taste of my own hypocrisy

rises like a bile within my soul

and like some poison of the spirit

pours out and overflows

thus freeing itself from an environment

where its evils and its failings

found not a happy home

but a nature more kind and righteous

than would be born witness by my wicked past

or the dark thoughts which sometimes

have given rise to bad behavior

and brought upon me such black stains

of despair and deepest shame.

Too Many Scars

They say I've got too many scars

to be less than thirty-five

but hell, I know I'm lucky

to even be alive

Death and Chaos came at me

from every way they could

and no one says I ran or hid

I went charging right on through

But now I'm not so young they say

used up all of my nine lives

but I just can't see backing down

or not living my own life

So let them come and get me

if it ever comes the day

But I refuse to be a follower

I'll live and die in my own way.

Scared of the Silence

Have I grown scared of the silence too

like all too many I know

Have I grown unaccustomed to the silence of the Night

the peace I once found in my soul

Have I, by living this modern city life

lost the serenity of silence, the love of time alone

or am I so ashamed that my everyday mind

hesitates and refrains to accept

the forgiveness of the soul?

The Fight Went On

She said

she wanted to see me

lying face down

in a urine soaked gutter.

What high ambitions

you have

I said.

The fight went on.

Dry Heaves

Had the dry heaves this morning

must be letting myself down

this running round and drinking

only brings me to the ground

And I'm trying through my dying

to stay close to the Light

but I'm crying in the morning

when I see my blood-stained eyes

And I don't even know the story

that this plot turns out to be

but these failures stop the glory

that maybe Life might bring to me

But I'm not heading for the chaos

I've seen that storm and felt that rain

I'm not gonna stray too far away

from the Source I'll need again

And I'm living in a dream world

with "what is" and "what could be"

And I'm hoping some sweet sister

gonna bring me to my feet

But I know that ain't the answer

the strength is here inside

and I only need the reason

to make it come alive

So I'm giving up self-pity

and I'm gonna go away

try to get my life together

and start again a brand new day.

Hopes of the Fallen

My silk handkerchief is torn now

just like all my fancy clothes

they have holes and rips, are faded

like the dreams I once held close

I guess I learned my lessons

they cost enough I know

All my money, pride, and dignity

were lost, not long ago

Cocaine took all my money

while alcohol took my pride

My dignity lost between them both

during my landslide of decline

But having reached the bottom

only three choices remain

to stay, to die, or go forward

and two of those the same

to stay here at the bottom

a coke-slave and a drunk

insures that Death's Dark Knight stands waiting

in the shadows close beside

But I've chosen to go forward

renew my body, soul, and mind

leave this deep pit of self-destruction

I'm still too alive to die.

Images of My Dreams

In the Sea of my mind

I sometimes catch the images of my Dreams

currents dark and cool

currents warm and sunny

and many are the creatures of my mind

some so beautiful and lovely

others are the facts I would forget

as pollution of a Sea unexorciseable

I feel the daily life a deathly trap

and seek the tinges of immortality

wrapped up in the intensity of the moment

I seek to risk my life - to foil my death

and having walked beside it, say I tried

but Life demanded of me life

as the Sea the waters of the river.

American Bar Scene

For the first, in way too long a time long a time

    I looked into a woman's eyes

To see what really lay behind

    the false facade I always find

        to find you

Too many lies in such short time

    too much deceit, and mostly mine

my dreams of warmth were left behind

    too much good cause for my decline

        I chose isolation

I hate to see the people where

    the cancerous smoke congests the air

and the lonely, horny masses huddle

    rubbing up against each other

looking for what they'll never find

   and settling for the best in line

     just like dogs fucking

and so the children of the Night

   seduced by alcohol's delights

do their dance without the Sun

   mostly from themselves they run

     to Darkness.

And I alone, a child of Night

   long seduced by the Moon's pale Light

had given up the useless fight

   yet failed to accept the human plight

     choosing to ignore it.

And now you sit in front of me

   you Light-filled eyes revives in me

a memory of forgotten dreams

reminds me of a life I've seen

    and died to.

But if we never meet again

    and if I never feel your hands

and if our bodies never merge

    to explore our minds' and bodies' worlds

at least for once in some dark room

    something almost spiritual, something good

shook me almost to Awake

    to realize that human fate

is not to be a cow or sheep

    but is what each one does, what each one makes

        of their own life.

Oblivion Disease

I don't want that knock me out number

    I don't have that oblivion disease

It's not that the Lord is coming back

    Or the missiles quelled for peace

But I don't have to put me out

    to lay me down to sleep

the war with myself is all but over

    and it's time for inner peace.

Easter Morning

Tomorrow's Easter morning, circa 1985

I haven't lived out all my dreams

but at least I'm still alive

I've seen the shit hit several times

and I've always fought on through

but self-discipline comes harder

as the grains of time slip through

and yet I still have several goals

that haven't changed along the way

and I try to live life harmlessly

till harm gets in my way

But I feel so strong my spirit's need

to shine brighter than before

inside I need to free my soul

and in my shining soar.

The Night Calls My Soul

Hungrily, tirelessly, the Night calls unto my soul

proffering that longed for peace of Darkness

But does peace lay hidden in the Darkness

or is that all illusion?

And if no man shall see the face of God and live

who did Jesus call his Daddy?

Will it all come down to dust

will echoes still be heard in Heaven

will the praises never end

or will they never be beginning

is the story to be told

or always moving

in the middle?

Going Into the Night

Every time I hear him on the radio

the king of blues

singing how he'll go out of his mind

or into the night

I can't help but smile

I've rushed into that Night

my whole life

and still, for all my life

I don't understand the night

Is Darkness good, is Darkness bad

I don't like evil

but I do love a secret to share

I like Mysteries, questions

something that's unresolved

and so it will remain

I love the stars, I love the Sky

I adore the Moon

I love the Night - I love the Night.

The Hours After Midnight

I love the hours after midnight

    and shadows cast by the Moon

I love the feel of the warm west wind

    wet across my face

and I love fog rolling in

    billowing off the water at night

And I love the inexpressible warmth

    which is a woman

sweating hotly

    in the cool of my night

I need to look into eyes so dark

    so deep, so impenetrable

that they reflect the Mystery

    which is Life

I love the lush green coolness

    of the wild forest

and the peace

    which engulfs me there

and I love to merge

    with Nature's wholeness

during the "little death"

    which pleasure brings.

Life and Death

Life is like a good and beautiful woman

      a joy and pleasure to make love with

Death is like a dark seductress of the Night

      with whom the strong flirt, but do not succumb.

Spiritual Warrior's Life-code

Receive everyone

      as you would want to be received

treat others

      as you would be treated

for they are an extension and individualization

      of the same One Life from which all springs

But if they grievously deceive you and hurt you

      and are injurious to those you love and protect

take them off at the knees

    without mercy.

Cycles of Desperation

There's a rhythm in how it comes and goes

    these cycles of desperation

when it's gone I'm calm, I'm dealing fine

    when it comes I'm half a madman

Sometimes I see and know the cause

    other times it slips up on me

but the pressure grows, the tension builds

    until some outlet or explosion.

Picking Up the Pieces

Picking up the pieces

    from a wild weekend

causes there's work to be done

    and it's time to begin

Picking up the pieces

    one by one again

trying to get it right

    trying to set things straight

till I go wild again

And its kind of like my love life

    its kind of like my world

I get things going my way for awhile

    and then hit some wall again

Now I'm picking up the pieces

    from a wild, too wild weekend

and its kind of like my heart

    that's been shattered, broken, shattered

time and time again

So now I'm picking up the pieces...

    time and time again.

Soul Dispossessed

My libido pushes me out

    into the Night

There's not much I can do

    about it

It's the intensity of the urges

    inside

that amazes

    those beside me.

The mask and Shadow

    deep inside

are not always proud

    or fond of one another

But still, a soul this dispossessed

    has got a lot of power

        driving, moving it.

And I call unto the soul

    within my Night

and Trust and Hope my Spirit

    is there waiting

But still, a soul this dispossessed

can have misunderstandings

    dealt by Nature

And still, I call unto the soul

    within my Night

while outside the morning birds

      start singing

they bring the promise of the message

      hoped for

a Soul reborn, a Soul's renewal.

Recklessness

The recklessness with which I've lived my life

has probably been the power that sustains it

if I were miserly-like to grasp on to Life

afraid every second I might lose it

then surely it would lose its' special flavor for me

and then surely, I would lose it.

Tortured Sleep of the Damned

I find myself awake at night

    as though I slept

the tortured sleep of the damned

What persecutes me

    this pain racked body

        and my own inability

            to fulfill myself wholly

Why is being our own selves

    the most difficult challenge

why doesn't anything set me fully free

    free in my Self

        free in my Being.

Touch of Time

I see the lightning on the Ocean

I feel lightning in my soul

I've stopped myself so many ways

Now I feel like I'll explode

I've recognized those things in life

that have stopped me every time

but it's not those things

but my weakness to them

which brought sorrow and decline

And now I'm home with Mother Ocean

She heals me every time

and renewed I feel I've much to give

and I feel the touch of Time.

Rend A Tear

I get a certain kind of peace from the ocean

    a deep and gentle rest

it must in a way be like dying

    except without the mess

I kind of sorta tried some times

    to make this hard life cease

But every time the Joys of Life

    harkened live, and be at peace

Yes I did do the Dance with Death

    laid with the lure of suicide

and I have spent way too many hours waiting

    loaded gun there beside me

But every time I made my choice

    and decided to live Life

yeah, every time I made my choice

    I decided to live Life

and though every day is filled with pain

      there is still the Joy of Life

and though I've seen it hit the fan

      too many times to count

and though my body's filled with scars

      I still do worship Life

and I will not give in this time

      I'll conquer, I'll survive

But still the anger, still the rage

      still the question why

but all that is a mental game

      of what and where and why

in truth, we speak of Power

      and I mean real Power, not that of greed

and I don't really give a shit

      about life's superficial games

If I had a chance

      I'd tear things up

and try to make things right

    but who the hell really gives a shit

and who has the balls to fight

But God in Heaven knows my name

    and I know his out loud

and the God and Goddess of all Life

    in my soul they do conspire

and I will rend a tear in it

    this veil that halts my way

and I will grow into full life

    Self-Aware and Self-Awake

And I will rend a tear in it

    this veil that blocks my path

And I would tear this world apart

    and try to make things right.

And rebuild from the heart.

Light In Darkness

In my own way

    I have been a shining light

    in utter darkness

Although the darkness in which I dwelled

    took its' toll on me

    and on my soul as well.

I Woke Up Screaming

I've woken up screaming

    in the middle of the night

    from this persistent pain

too many nights

    I've woken myself up screaming

That is life, at least a part of life,

    for me.

But that is not all my life consists of

      for the joy outweighs the sorrow

I see the love and light

      in my two year old niece's eyes

and that's all the joy I need

      all I need to survive.

Anything

Alcohol's had a hold on me

      for too, too long a time

I didn't realize

      just how strong

till I'd left it far behind

My eyes are clear

      I see real life

not the blur of life

    I'd made

and now I know

    with full certainty

I can accomplish anything.

From Heart to Hand

Poetry

    is the basis

of my sanity

    I have to write.

From heart to hand

    my soul

    as spirit flies

seeking release

    of what is right

long chained up

    deep inside

From heart to hand

    my soul

    as spirit flies

seeking that

    sweet union

    with The Good

that patiently waits inside

        as in all things

from heart to hand

    my soul

    as spirit

    flies

uniting

    what is Dark

    within my soul

with what is Light

from heart to hand

    my soul

    in spirit

    flies

and brings me

    both release

    and peace

and helps to keep

    things right.

Hope

Hope, walking along

the outside wall

looking in

It is the time of my re-awakening.

World Gone Mad

They're starting to find bodies

    in my parent's neighborhood

one here, one there

    over the years

Is no place safe?

Must crime reach out

    and touch the innocents

or are there no innocents left

    in a world gone mad?

Play With Death

Alcohol, drugs, and danger

    are just stupid ways to play with death

vainly trying to count coup

    on what we cannot conquer, nor comprehend

We are so scared of Death's Power

    that we strike

out at its' form

    but we all know

        that Death is mandatory

It's a door

    we all pass through.

Still Living When

        Maybe I'm still living

      when the Allman Brothers were king

      and the streets were full of love

         and revolution

        Maybe I still seek to see

       mini-skirted hippy women

beautiful breasts bouncing freely

in those halters

Maybe I still feel like

and think to be seventeen

Maybe I was born

for revolution

with so much change

so much change gone down

can it really be

my age has doubled.

Suicide's A Waste

It's the first clear night since New Year's

for almost two weeks straight

its been rain, death, and funerals

I could use some relief

Two of my relatives

two of my friends

and two strangers across the street

a strange woman killed her retarded son

and then she killed herself

I guess she couldn't sleep

Depression must be a hard thing

I've come my own hard way

and I may have thought about it

and I may have played with it

but suicide's a waste.

Your Choices

You can either

    run away from life

Embrace it

or conquer it.

Those are your choices.

Tired of the Waste

I'm getting tired of seeing lost souls

seeing the self-tortured damned

    its not artistic

    its not dramatic

    it's just a total waste

    a waste of time

    a waste of life

    it's just a stupid total waste

I want to be with

    the contributors

    not with the polluted flotsam and jetsam

    tossed about by Life's strong waves.

Hold on to Strength

Once you accept the thought

    that you're a weak fuck

you become one

    Hold on to your strength

your pride, your inner being

    hold on to yourself

hold on to inner strength.

Because if you give those things away

    to someone else's harmful thoughts

what is left

    and what will come to replace them.

I Believe

I believe in the beauty

    and the dignity

and the basically heroic spirit

of the human being.

I believe in Love.

I believe in us.

Kiss the Sky

It's a silent rain

      falling outside

the raindrops drop

      without much weight

barely kissing

      as they touch the Earth

From Sky to Earth

      their journey made.

But me

      when I fell

            I fell heavy

over seven stories

       they say

and me, when I fell

       I fell heavy

taking so much

       of my life away.

So now I sit

       and look up skyward

I want to jump

       then soar and fly

and reverse these raindrops

       gently falling

to fly from Earth

       and kiss the Sky.

Modern Urban Landscape

The modern urban landscape

is much like the hunter's woods

there is danger in the darkness

there are shadows filled with death

But the hunter hunts to feed himself

and his family there at home

hunters don't hunt within their species

he only kills to bring food home

the dealers prey on the youth and ghettos

the dealers prey on their own friends

and dealers, like fierce wild animals

so territorial they fight and kill

this modern landscape

a dangerous landscape

much worse than the hunter's woods

in the hunter's woods

just food is taken

in the city they kill

for drugs and greed.

No Sympathy for Some Suicides

I have no sympathy

    for the weak hearted

who take their lives in vain

to do so as an act of strength or mercy

    is one thing

to do it in sadness

    in weakness

    in desperation

that is something else.

Love the Night

Much like the mythical vampires of old

    I love the Night

and like the mythical werewolves of old

    I need the Night

and like the coven under the Moon

    I work the Night.

Yes, I love the Night

I Embrace and work the Night.

I <u>work</u> the Night.

Howl in the Moonlight

Sometimes when I look up at the Moon at night

I smile

    and then I howl in the Moonlight

        howl in the Moonlight

        I howl in the Moonlight

        howl in the Moonlight

I know I have a beast inside

    an animal both fierce and wild

not in any way bad or evil

    it's just wild and free

        free and full of life

      so I howl in the Moonlight

        howl in the moonlight

I run low in the shadows

    and I howl in Moonlight

        howl in the Moonlight

because I'm free

    and I'm alive

I howl in the Moonlight

howl in the Moonlight.

Guns and Hormones

Raging hormones

    and guns

    just don't mix

No adolescent male

    with a bad temper

    and hormones raging

    needs a gun

no outraged housewife

    no jealous husband

    no irate lover

    needs a gun

guns and raging hormones

    equals death

    equals carnage

    equals suicide

    equals murder

guns and raging hormones

    just don't mix.

When

  When can the strong be weak

      when can the self-sufficient be lonely

when can the strong be weak

      when can the humble find glory.

The Golden Green

I know lots of now ex-hippies

    that still smoke the golden green

they might not let their bosses know

      unless their bosses do the same

but green is better than the drink

      the drink takes too many lives

the green it is a peaceful herb

      the drink is liquid fire

mystics all around the world

      have used the golden green

while every kind of human being

      has been ruined by the drink.

Why

I had a friend

      who died

when he passed out dead-drunk

      in the back of a pickup truck

in Texas

      somehow he cut the circulation off

      to his brain

I've had friends

      who died

when they fell 150 feet with me

      I woke up

           why

I've had friends

      that died of cancers

I've had friends

      that died of strokes

I've got a friend

      with shrapnel in his head

from Vietnam

      his head sets off

security alarms

I've had friends

    that died

in stupid, useless car wrecks

    I've got friends

        too many friends

            who've died

some so needless

    some so stupid

I just have to wonder

    Why?

        Why?

            Why?

After A Carwreck

Now I'm feeling all this anger

Now I'm feeling all this shame

How could I be so careless

and hurt my body once again

I'd done so well for so long

Now I feel just like a fool

What will it take to teach me

to give in and follow rules

I'm feeling kind of stupid

I'm feeling kind of lame

I don't know what I was thinking

didn't know I was insane

I was feeling like a kid again

I was feeling really young

So I drove just like a wildman

like the madman I'd become

And now I lay in bed in pain

and I wear this silly cast

And I wonder for the millionth time

why did I drive so fast.

Death Wish

You Know I never wrecked a car

when I was driving with a passenger

but by myself

I've wrecked too many cars to count

what is the lesson here

do I care about others

more than I do myself

do I have no self-discipline

when by myself

Do I have to push the limits

is it lack of self-control

or just bad luck and timing

or a death wish in my soul.

Moderation and Extremes

Some of us

    have extremes

        within our

            moderation

Some of us

    have moderation

        within our

            extremes.

Crosses and Abuses

We've all got our crosses to bear

maybe yours is heavier than mine

maybe it isn't

    that's all relative, very relative

we all know pain and suffering

    we all know joy and happiness

and that's enough

    unless somebody's pain and suffering

is your joy and happiness

    and then something's wrong, very wrong

As I watch the news

      and hear the news

I see the murders, rapes, and suicides

      I see anger and a need

      for justice

What is wrong with us, I wonder

      just what is wrong?

Indian Soul

I was born American

      a little bit of everything

I'm Scottish, and Irish, and Cherokee, and Creek

      I've always lived my life wild and free

I've got an Indian Soul

In my heart and in my mind

    I'd rather live a natural life

with love and respect for Mother Earth

    than the way we use, while Nature hurts

I've got an Indian Soul

From my head down to my toes

    I've got an Indian Soul.

Hot Eyes, Cold Blue Steel

I've seen

    hot eyes

and cold blue steel

I've heard desperate lies

    in a quicksand field

I've felt the

                        muscles harden

waited for

                        the hammer to fall

feeling for

                        the coming bullet

waiting for

                        the damage done

I've looked at

    truthful eyes

hearing

    lying words

I've seen the

    backstab coming

while I

    still held on firm

I've seen the

    brick wall rushing

and did not

      hit the brakes

I heard the

      gun exploding

but by then

      was way too late

I've waited

      in my kitchen

with an M-1

      set to kill

I've seen those

      hot eyes flashing

wrapped my hand

      round cold blue steel

I've heard my

      lover howling

when we

      stole the Moon

and I've felt the

      whiplash crushing

didn't flinch

      but crashed on through.

Come and Share My Sickness

He said

      come and share my sickness

I was handed

      my first drink

Someone said

      come and share my sickness

and I learned

      some violent things

She said

      come and share my sickness

and she taught me

      to snort coke

they always want

      to share their sickness

it's the least

      they can afford

they say

      come and share my sickness

cause it hates

      to be alone

they call

      come and share my sickness

to the weak

      and to the strong

they say

      come and share my sickness

they don't want

      to sin alone

they say

      come and share my sickness

until in you

      its found a home

they say

      come and share my sickness

with a needle

      or a gun

they say

      come and share my sickness

some TV preacher

      selling souls

he says

      come and share my sickness

and please send

      your money in

they say

      come and share my sickness

they can't be alone

      with just themselves

Well I say

      hell no to their sickness

to the violence

      and the greed

I say

      hell no to their sickness

people die

      for damn cocaine

I say

      hell no to their sickness

skid row

      does not need me

I say

      hell no to their sickness

it's in yourself

      you must believe.

Dark Corners of Her Soul

She saw him

    when he walked into the room

he had death wish

    written all over his face

There was something

    in the dark corners

        of her soul

that responded to him

    she wasn't drawn

to the soft and steady lifestyle

    to her that daily life

seemed a deathly boring trap

    she was unconsciously

        drawn to danger

it pulled at her

    like a river does

        a floating leaf

She did not

    waste time

        in nothings

a few short words

    was all

        it took

their attraction was natural and animal

    and to her

was real and good.

Mellow Fellow

He was a vary mellow fellow

he didn't get upset

he knew his life had highs and lows

and every wave must have its crest

he had a quiet and gentle power

he never made a scene

he navigated the waves Life sent at him

with a rudder never seen.

What Fine Webs

What fine webs

we humans weave

of human bondage

and deceit

the way we dance

and play and flirt

with our own lives

with our own hearts.

What purpose is there

we must cry

as whirling on the floor

we fly

into the tangled webs

we weave

of human bondage

and deceit.

Savagery of Love - the Lust for Justice

Let's talk about the savagery of Love

and love's protectors

what wouldn't you do

to defend your child or loved one

let's talk about what's basic

what's deep inside

in the reptilian mind-core

that primal animal in your mind

let's talk about love and protection

about what you wouldn't do

let's talk about the savagery of love

and what you would and wouldn't do.

Ode to the Outlaws

She was no pox-ridden road whore

    not to say she ain't been around

he was no angel his-self

    seen him lots of rough stuff go down

he was a felon just jumped bail

    she rode a danger-jones monkey

neither were scared of prison or pain

    both of 'em outlaw by nature

They couldn't go no other way

    they couldn't see the need

they ran at life on full throttle

    they'd never see their old age

fires like they've got

    always burn way too hot

        and lives like they lead

            just seem destined to bleed

                and won't leave nothing behind

                    but their seed.

\

Rebel Bred

I ain't no coal miner's daughter

ain't no gator got my granny

and my first cousins didn't marry

but that don't mean we didn't party

Yeah I'm rebel born and rebel bred

but that ain't got nothing to do with hate

don't have nothing to do with racism

that ain't the southern gentleman's way

I'm proud to be a southern man

at least we learned some decent manners

learned to live this life with grace

and in harmony with Nature.

Prey or Predator

I hear the hawk hunting outside

    diving for the kill

am I like the prey or predator

    in this life that seems unreal

I don't want to hurt nobody

    but I'm tired of being hurt

I'm tired of hurting on the inside

    and living with this pain

I don't feel I'm being preyed upon

    and I sure don't want to kill

or make my way by walking

    on the gentle in this world

I don't feel this modern greed or hate

    I guess it's just not in my soul

maybe I was born to be a warrior

    of Spirit, not of blood.

Urges Aren't Frantic

Baby sleeping in the next room

      time to do Tai Chi

I guess my life is mellowing

      and maybe that's okay

I'm tired of risks and danger

      now I like to get my sleep

now I love my nieces and nephews

      instead of tools of cold blue steel

Maybe that's part of ageing

      I'm finally growing up

maybe it's the hormones

      maybe its old blood

but those urges aren't as frantic

      as once took hold of me

and the self-discipline gets easier

      and so does finding peace.

Political, Historical, and Social Commentary

These poems are comments on various subjects or events, and presented in a loosely chronological order. They are self-explanatory if not always consistent. They tend to represent an emotional reaction or outburst. They are not well thought out positions, just comments.

1981-1985

American

I have a right to be free

    because I am an American

I have the right to be free

    and I'm thankful I'm an American

But if the government has the right

    to ask me for me (as in a military draft)

I have a right

    to expect certain things back

If I pay taxes for an education

    it had better be a good education

        that is free, fair, and responsive

I have a right to expect the government

    to give me good value

        for the money I contribute

I have a right to pursue happiness and enjoy privacy

    a right to not be stopped, or searched, or hassled

        for the way I look or the opinions I keep

I have a right to be free

    and I am thankful I'm an American

although America is FAR from sinless

I'm glad I'm an American.

Perfect Piece

Everybody in America

    everybody, everywhere

chasing in their conditioned minds

    that perfect piece of ass

Everywhere you turn

    that dream is rammed right down your throat

to chase, to seek, to find, to have

    that perfect piece of ass

And though the satisfaction's nil

    the chase is with us, ever still

and both the sexes wink and stare

    or sit alone at home and stare

    at blank white walls while wishing for

        that perfect piece of ass

It's as American as apple pie

        it's as French as French champagne

there's no true style, just what we're fed

        in every culture, everywhere

and we continue without thinking

        that quest, that search, that ever seeking

for that perfect piece of ass

        the three scars on the native's face

a small or big bust - what's in style

        it matters not the place or time

all wrongly sell the superficial

        stand it up as all important

make it something on the mind

        that perfect piece - that golden prize.

Progress

I hear the sound of bulldozers

      killing, clearing away the trees

           and I hate it

As I always have.

I drove one for a time

      but I tore up buildings, not forests

           and I felt okay, but it's not the same

I'm for the human race and survival

      and I know people have to live somewhere

           and you can't stop progress

I just hope there's something left

      besides concrete.

Home

I smell the wet grass of Georgia

    and I know that I am home

I see white oaks spreading under a full and exquisite Moon

    and I love Her

I've rode, flown, and sailed

    towards the bending of the Earth

As far as I could

    but I always came home

I could have the riches of Swiss land

    the golden sun of Mexico

the clear cool Caribbean

    and I'd still come home

I could have a harem in Morocco

    or a temple in Tibet

and I'd still come home

Home is where the Earth

    flows into your soul without separation

home is where the newly broken soil

    feels and smells right

Home is where there are still

    more trees and forests

than anything else

    and there always better be

Your Home is worth living for

    and one of the very few things

worth killing or dying for

    Home.

Choice

We've got to clean this world up

    not feel destined to destroy it

my generation started so much change

    the whole world's in need of changing

we have the potential to end life here on Earth

    or the ability to improve its quality

Its time to act our age as a species

    our singular gift is our intelligence

we've got to use our minds and cooperate

    for unilateral nuclear disarmament

there is no physical obstacle to this task

    just a lack of human competence

its time the people and wills of nations

    erased this danger to ourselves

it has fallen on this time in history

    to choose Life over Death irrevocably.

1982 Surprise

George Wallace just got elected by the black vote

    has everything gone crazy

or has integration worked down home

    in the land below the mason

The fifties to the eighties

    hasn't been but thirty years

but the lion and the sheep lay down together

    with the others in the field

maybe the world is getting better

    in both big and little ways

and integration has really worked now

    in a land once tilled by slaves.

Change

You say there ain't much change since '64

but I know that isn't true

its really worlds and worlds that's changed

in less than thirty years

Remember the hatred and the bigotry

right out front for all to see

we've come a long, long way since then

we've come a long, long way

America can stand up proud

South Africa should look and see

all races can live in harmony

by law and on the streets.

1985-1987

Que San

I remember praying for the men at Que San

They spent 82 days in Hell

I was 14, didn't know about war

But I prayed as hard as I can

a new generation comes up today

they don't remember the blood and gore

they're watching movies, playing macho

they'll get their chances soon

our world's conditions will see to that, you know they always do

they'll get their taste of war soon enough

its sad but they always do.

Long Tine Gone

I saw a movie called the big chill

I've felt that chill for years

tonight that coolness stung my ears

and brought this man to tears

did we all get bought off, or just sell out

or fucking die along the way

I'm thirty-one and crying out

like I did at 17

I don't see why it had to stop

or slow down along the way

the chill is nothing but cold greed

that picks us off along the way.

Rocked the World

You can say my generation got bought off

or you can say we're the generation that tried

we carried banners pleading love and peace

while the other half of us fought and died

although we didn't find a lasting peace

we'll not apologize

we could not make humanity grow up

but we made some change in time

as a generation we've been ridiculed

and we're still misunderstood

but from '65 to '75

you know we rocked the world.

A Thousand Points of Light

(George Bush - 1988)

They say

    he sees a thousand points of Light

God I hope he does

    Because those points of Light

        were already out there

        and I pray to God we're used

For I do want

    a kinder America

        and more gentle Americans

And I strongly want a clean environment

    and an America I can be proud of

        like all peoples in Nature

            we've certainly made our mistakes

yet America still stands for Freedom

    we still let freedom ring

        for individuality and equality

    we still let freedom ring

        for individuality, justice, and equality.

    we still let freedom ring.

1988-1992

In the Ricefields

There were no protestors there

    when they swept the streets of Que

There were no peace-niks in the ricefields

    they were all safe far away

It's so damn easy

    to condemn

what's in a distant land

and ignore the wrongs

you see

before you

at the distance of your hand

The men who fought and died there

did not create that war

did not decide to fight there

didn't begin a brand new war

there was a treaty

S.E.A.T.O.

and a government failing

and under siege

from the threats without

and from the threats within

And America sent Her Warriors

to defend Freedom

    once again

And they never lost one single conventional battle

  while the politicians lost the war

the Warriors came home undefeated

  while the politicians lost the war.

Viet Nam Remembered

The men with guns were not in Congress

  the men with Purple Hearts

    and scars

      and missing limbs

the men who took

  that last silent ride

    wrapped inside a body bag

They were not in Congress

  they were not President

they didn't refuse to declare a war

    they just fought and died in it

they didn't give a damn

    about the polls or upcoming elections

they simply fought

    and stayed alive or died

        they did their jobs with courage

God bless them all

God bless them all.

Like They Should Have

        I killed the bastard

        like they should have

        said the father

        of the molested child

        now they want to give me

        his place in jail.

Spring Coming

The Spring is coming

I can see the buds on the trees

the spring is coming

I can see flowers rising up through the leaves

the spring is coming

Freedom flowers in eastern Europe

the spring is coming

Freedom flashes in China too

the spring is coming

Nelson Mandela's is finally sprung free

the spring is coming

Freedom's flowers blossoms so sweet

the spring is coming

everywhere freedom flowers sweet.

The Murder Of Innocence

I knew the bountiful dreams of childhood

    the dreams of an innocent youth

I hope that still exists today

    or are the dreams of innocence gone

is innocence now a thing of the past

    lost at way too early an age

and is this the result of urban chaos

    or the fault of the TV/Media Age

I don't know why its gone

I don't know how it happened

and I don't know any way to punish

those who murdered priceless innocence.

Early 70's - Status Test/Acid Test

I remember when

      in high school times

those who tried

      but couldn't pass

the status test

      fell down and out

and many passed

      the acid test

which came in time

      to simply mime

the status test

but many got lost

      and some took their lives

because they could not

      could not find

some way to make it

      and get on by

in each and everyone

      it seems

we have a need to be

      and to achieve

a need that must be met and passed

to simply go on.

Viet Nam and Now - Stand Tall for Freedom

You know I can't forget

      the bloodshed of '68

      the Chicago convention in '68

      the burning summer of '65

and I can't forget all the changes

made in so little time

there was so much being rammed at us back then

and so much we gave back

half of us serving and dying

half of us hunting ass

I can remember my sweet mother

she offered a ticket north

she said I'd rather see you run away

than die in that foreign land

As it went, no choice ever came down

although I cried hard in '71

my brother drew number 14 to go

they said he was gone and done for sure

then Nixon changed his mind again

as he so often did

he wanted to kick somebody's ass

but he didn't know how or who or when

Me, I thought I was ready

but then they said no way

at 17, two felony drug convictions

meant a criminal, not soldier's fate

then my body got wrecked here at home

and so I suffered on through

with the rest of a country in chaos

mislead by leaders who misunderstood

We finally pulled out of Asia

it was never a practical war

although thousands fought and died there

all we had was shattered hope

The gooks were so incredibly corrupt

to them we were out of place

but America keeps on fighting, fighting

I hope for Freedom

anytime and anyplace

in this world

who else is willing

to lay it on the line

to fight for Freedom

who else is willing

anyplace and any time.

Advice to the Streets

God damn it

    You know jail is miserable

really miserable

    and I'm not even talking down the road for years

I'm saying jail, in hours, days, weeks

or months

is miserable.

Just not worth it.

    Not fucking worth it.

So whatever law you don't like

    change it

        before you break it

    cause going down the road

        it really sucks

        it really sucks

I've hurt every day of my life since 1972

    every fucking day

but I believe Life is beautiful, I don't complain

    cause two people bought it

    on the same fall I fell

and I'm glad to be here

    it beats being dead

and God knows I'm a live wire

    I'm more than alive

my life's not gravy

    and there's so much I desire

sure, my body hurts me

    but I'm not alone

I'm not doing twenty - to - life

    or without food or home

I'm not a slave to a needle

    I'm not boosting with a gun

so my life's not too bad

    it's much better than some

But I have a secret

      called spirit and will

and I know I'll conquer

      it comes with the will.

1991 - So Far, So Good

the winds of war

      are blowing through Arabia

America kicking ass

      trying, after so long

to make the U.N. work

to give world consensus

      real teeth

and its going great

      so far, so good

if you're American

    and you like to win

its going great

    so far, so good

and for the Arab world as well

    so far, so good

one less regional threat

    so far, so good.

Crack is Evil

I don't really need

    to hear the grass grow

or have my heart

    pounding against my chest

I don't need to smoke cocaine

    the devil likes that freebase mess

the devil created crack cocaine

    it's a plague on the USA

the devil loves to see them smoke

    smoke and waste their lives away.

God In Man

Tears come to my eyes

    every time

I hear Martin Luther King's "I have a Dream" speech

    and I know God is Good

and I know God is Love

and that the love and good in man

    is God in man

praise God, which is all Good in Life

    and praise be to Life

when Good, and Love, and Truth

    flow from any man

as they did Martin Luther King.

Serve Each Other

In a more perfect society

    whether obliquely or overtly

we would all serve each other

    and recognizing that

respect each other

    for whatever service

is rendered

    one unto the other.

Antietam Creek

I think about Antietam Creek

    where the blood turned water red

where cornfields could be walked across on bodies

    never once would feet touch ground

I think about brothers and cousins

fighting in the fields

each side believing they were right

while the only victor was Death's Dark Knight.

1992 - God Bless Bill Clinton

God bless Bill Clinton

    he's got it tough

so many hot spots

    all over the globe

so many homeless

    so many - no jobs

its time to make changes

    this is *our* time

our parents did well before us

    now we seek to do what's right

America should keep getting better

    its finally *our* time.

America the Free

200 years of Freedom

    America the free

Oliver Stone claims one coup-de-tat

    but still democracy reigns free.

200 years of democracy

    an example for the rest

we the people govern

    that's the way it works the best.

Alas Columbia

I see starlight

    twinkling through the oak trees

and I know that life is good

    for too long I let a shadow lay upon me

my mistake

    still, the judge misunderstood.

I was thinking about Columbia

    that Latin land down by the sea

and how things were so much better there

    when sister Herb was queen

it was a gentler, saner world then

    in that land down by the sea

when herb was their main export

    long before cocaine was king.

Blue Berets

I salute the soldiers of peace

    the soldiers of Mother Earth

I salute the U.N. troops

    who fight that peace might work

I salute the soldiers of peace

    and those light blue berets worn with pride

I pray we use rightly these soldiers of peace

    whenever the need arise.

1992-1995

Tired of the Gripers

I'm tired of hearing actors

    complain about their jobs

what could be easier

    the jails are filled with actors

every liar is an actor

    every con man is an actor

every trial lawyer is an actor

    what could be easier

I'm tired of hearing musicians

      complain about their job

what could be easier

      than playing music every night

and living life as one long party

I'm tired of hearing athletes

      complain about their jobs

what could be easier

      than playing the sport you love

and getting paid way too damn much to do it

      what the hell could be easier

I'm tired of hearing people

      gripe about their jobs

they're damn lucky to have one

the people who have the <u>right</u> to gripe

      are the hard sweating minimum wagers

the poorly paid people doing the physical work

      while the rich keep getting richer.

Nostradamus

The dejavu of destruction

      he saw it as a dream

in the visions of Nostradamus

      he foretold such horrible things

and the predicted time is coming

      will those changes come to be

in the vision of Nostradamus

      there's great war before great peace

is this the dejavu of destruction

      will those horrors come to be

is it all a hollow warning

      or will there be chaos then world peace?

Cleaning House

Society used to put the pedophiles

    in the regular prison population

where they'd get killed

    it was a system that worked.

now our society has degenerated

    so badly

        that in this state

            they have a prison

just for bad cops and sex offenders.

I say put the bad cops

    and the child molesters

        back in the big house

and let Nature take its course.

Thirty Thousand Murders by Sixteen

When will modern humanity

    take some responsibility

for the images it creates

we show our children

    30,000 murders

        by the time they turn 16

what do we expect them

    to become

        other than murderers

have they been shown

    even 100 acts

        of unconditional love

to offset the impact

    of 30,000 murders.

Atlanta's Uglification

I watch the woods shrink

    around Atlanta

and it makes me sad

    it makes me mad

where will all the animals go

    they just die off

with no place to live.

Aren't the humans

    and their behavior

        ugly enough

            without destroying

All of God's true beauty - Nature.

Trees of My Childhood

They're cutting down

      the trees of my childhood

trees I climbed

      trees I built tree houses in

it's so sad to me

      how all the woods are dying

all the natural habitats are shrinking

      not because modern man

needs a place to live

      but because modern builders

have no sense of aesthetics

      of the beauty of Nature

of the serenity of the forest

      instead the builders build

and build and overbuild

      instead of leaving wooded areas

and the native wildlife's habitats

      they overbuild and overbuild

in every wooded lot

      until no woods are left

just suburbs, strip malls, parking lots

      until no woods are left at all

and it's too late

      and the beauty is gone.

Children have an intrinsic <u>need</u> to interact with Nature

      to learn about and play in Nature

kids need woods and creeks

      and natural wildlife

to teach them about the lessons of life

      they need to see more

than domesticated dogs and cats

      which are now just extensions of humans

they need more than animals in the zoos

      they need to play in woods

they need to learn to commune with Nature.

To take away what is intrinsically needed by children

      for senseless overdevelopment

is a sin against children

      a sin against Nature

and a sin against God.

Concrete America

The continuity of our woodlands destroyed

      the legacy of modern man

of urban/suburban builders

      so thoughtless

with no eye to tomorrow

      where will the children climb and play

in what creeks will they catch the crawfish

      in what woods will they hear the owl

how can they see the hawk

      if he no longer has any prey left

I get madder and madder

    at the sound of bulldozers ripping up trees

I hate to see the woodlands destroyed

    the landscape devastated

for no other reason than greed

    pure greed

it would be so easy

    so easy

to mandate that for every so many houses

    they had to retain so much in woodlands

so much in wildlife sanctuaries

    for humanity can live in harmony with the land

nurture it and watch over it

    or mankind can destroy it

with no sense of aesthetics

    with no eye to the future

no concern for the children

    no concern for the wildlife

no concern for our Mother.

Earthsongs/Goddessongs

This section sings the praises of Mother Nature, Mother Earth, and the importance of the struggle to keep the greedy and shortsighted from doing irrevocable damage to our Mother and all our relations on this tiny, beautiful blue-green planet.

Earth Reborn

At 3:30 in the morning

    the spring air feels cool and soft

the dogwood trees are blooming now

    Christ's nailholes in a cross

the Beauty of the Springtime

    as the Earth renews its life

is a beauty that surpasses words

    and can best be praised in heart.

The Rites of Springtime call me

      as does the lush green woods

that my heart belongs to Nature

      I have always understood

so tonight I marvel at Her

      as I marvel every year

at the Beauty of our Mother Earth

      as She renews Herself again.

Her Love Transcends

I don't think

      anyone much

understands the way I think

      the visions visited

      the mystic peaks

but I can't comprehend

      what I cannot understand

I just follow on

    the Goddess

for Her love, it does transcend.

Summer Symphony

Summer sings its symphony

    in the crickets' song at night

an all pervading melody

    Nature taking flight

for although its Summer

    full and green

Autumn's close behind

    and then dark Winter's stillness

till Spring once more

    renews Her Life.

Call of the Heat

It's been raining here in Georgia

    Autumn's leaves have tired

the cold wet winds are coming

    I feel that I may have to fly.

I appreciate the cold clean air

    as Mother Nature takes a bath

the cold is cleansing and invigorating

    still, I yearn for what is hot.

I have so much work left to finish

    so many projects yet undone

but the hot sere wind and ocean winds

    do beckon to me, come.

Natural Meditation

Looking at the Ocean is a meditation

It lets you clear your mind and think

It teaches with beauty, Nature's wisdom

For observing Nature is the key

The Creator and Creation

    and the Created interplay

        we should watch, and look, and listen

            learn Nature's wisdom, pure and free

For the Stars and Space

the sea and land

the Sun, and Moon, and Sky

Are really all the books we need

If we learn their lessons right.

Miss the Caribbean

I miss the sweet smell of the Caribbean

    the warm glow of the Moon at night

light shimmering on the water

    a million waves reflecting her light

the whirling of our Mother turning

    the pull of the Goddess, the Queen of the Night

the pull upon the blue-green waters

    whose rhythms calm and lull the night

Our Queen the Moon ruling majestic

    the sky vault twinkling, bright myriad lights

I miss the rhythm of waves crashing

    the shimmering Moon on the water at night

I miss the clear and cool Caribbean

    I miss the Moon on the Ocean at night.

Brother Crow

My brother the Crow

    comes back to visit

I love to watch him fly and play

    he adapts

        to all his worlds

            so well

they say he sees the astral light

Brother Crow has time to play

    dancing with his friend the wind

Brother Crow has his tribe

        and family

not unlike his brother man.

Winter Cleansing

I won't stay here through the winter cleansing

    I find it too damn bleak

my life needs a bright southern sun

    and a warm sweet tropical breeze.

I have no love for frigid winter

    the autumn makes me sad

when autumn's leaves turn from red to brown

    and fall off to the ground

soon comes the cold of winter's cleansing

    its a cold I do not seek

that dreary bleak of winter's cleansing

    is something I'll not seek.

Hear the Song of Life

I hear the song of Life

    in the humming of a fan

I hear the song of Life

    as the leaves dance on the wind

I hear the song of Life

    in the pounding of the surf

I hear the song of Life

    in the echo finally heard

I hear the song of Life

    with my lover as she moans

I hear the song of Life

    as the babe first fills his lungs

I hear the song of Life

    sung by everything I see

I hear the song of Life

    as it sings to you and me

I hear the song of Life

      and its primal chord is love

I hear the song of Life

      and it calls me to be more

I hear the song of Life

      across this planet bathed in love

I hear the song of Life

      sung by this Earth, our Mother/home

I hear the song of Life

      and its primal chord is love

the song of Life is everywhere

      and the roots of Life are love.

Learn More From Nature

I'll learn more today

    by looking at the shape of a tree

then I will from a book

I'll hear more in the cawing of the crow

    then I will on the radio

Man surrounds himself

    with his insular world

choking on his self-made inadequacies.

Nature smiles on in perfection.

Prefer the Reservation

I prefer the Reservation

    although there's more to do out here

I prefer the reservation

    there's not much bullshit way out there

I prefer the reservation

    where my ancestors had to flee

to not be butchered by the whiteman

    driven crazy by his greed

I prefer the reservation

    I don't accept your obscene creeds

I reject your games and bullshit

    for my Mother beckons me

I won't buy into your program

    of pure self-serving greed

I reject your blatant bullshit

    my Mother bleeds and beckons me.

In Love With the Earth

I fall in love with the Earth

    everywhere I go

I fall in love with the Earth

    her beauty enamors me so

Whether it's the desert sky

    or the jungle's luscious glow

the beauty of a flower wild

    or a garden tended with love

I fall in love with the deep blue sky

    in love with the lightning flash

I love the storm, I love the thunder

    I love the smell of grass

And if this makes me a simple man

or simply uncivilized

then I plead guilty to being a barbarian

and loving Mother nature with great pride.

Earthsongs

I sing the Earthsongs

she needs her singers

I sing the Earthsongs

she needs her workers

I sing the Earthsongs

she needs her fighters

I sing the Earthsongs

she needs her lovers

I sing the Earthsongs

against the smog and grime

I sing the Earthsongs

against the sleaze and crime

I sing the Earthsongs

for the forests disappearing

I sing the Earthsongs

against your all-pollution

We don't have to poison ourselves

or the air we breathe

We don't have to scum up

every river and lake

We don't have to dump garbage

in the ocean deep

We don't have to do so much

that gets done every day

I sing the Earthsongs

there's got to be a better way

I sing the Earthsongs

there is a better way.

Must be Stopped

They're killing 150 elephants each day

    it must be stopped

they're killing rhinoceros every day

    it must be stopped

They're killing the whales and dolphins too

    it must be stopped

Somebody somewhere's got to do

    whatever it takes

        it must be stopped.

Walk With Beauty

I want to go back to the reservation

    it's not so crazy there

they still honor Mother Earth's Beauty

    they still commune with Nature there

and though the army's and settler's guns

    drove them to the roughest habitats in the country

they still sing and praise all Nature's glory

    and walk the sacred Earth with Beauty.

Used to Be

Didn't there used to be

    trees around here

didn't it used to be green

I thought I remember

    majestic tall oaks

        I thought I remembered

            great trees.

Snow

Snow is silent

    falling gently

Snow is silent, quite like death

Snow is silent

    snow is peaceful

like a quiet and restful death.

Hate the Destroyers

Tell me how

    not to hate

        the destroyers of Nature

tell me why

    I should forgive

       their carnal greed

   their unfortuitous

      shortsightedness

they doom their grandchildren

   they doom their children

      they doom us all

         all who breathe.

Natural Connection

I hear the sound of souls set free

   I feel my power growing

I feel the Earth groan and shake

   beneath me

and I feel Her power yearning.

The connections of the Soul denied

Modern Man, the blind one screaming

binds himself with chains of mind

    insulates himself from Mother Nature.

His source and other half cut off

    the light-being lost by his own choosing

modern man is merely shadow

    only half of his potential.

In the shadow lays light dormant

    the Light which strives to make Darkness visible

like the star's light seen alone at Night

    it's an inner light just half-way visible.

Care for Our Mother

Children are the joy of Life

    it's the way its always been

there is an intrinsic goodness

    in the process

of continuing life on Earth.

But now human families must expand

      the way they look at Life and plan things

we need a planet for our children

      with a higher quality of living.

Our sins against the Mother remain

      many of them must cease

its time to end our sad neglect

      and love and care for Mother Earth.

Advice to the Builder from Mother Earth

I look at the woods in contrast

      to the houses that intrude

those monsters known as suburbs

      eating up the oak tree's rule

and I cry inside each time I see it

      another stand of Oak trees down

why can't they let them be

      let the beauty stand, and build around.

Dawn Songbirds

The birds are singing outside

the dawn's breaking into day

the birds they sing the song of Life

another brand new day

the daybirds love to see dawn come

they love the sun to rise

cause night's dark fears do disappear

dissolved by glorious light.

Death of the Beauty

I hear and watch

    the bulldozers

        ripping up the woods

            where I played

                as a kid

God it makes me mad and sad

    God it makes me sick

        the beauty of this city fleeing

            going all too quick

with every oak tree felled

    this city looses

    bit by bit

    with every loss of Nature

    this city looses

    bit by bit.

A Prayer for Light

Great Spirit

    Mother Father Creator of All Life

Bless me

    May the light of the Father Sun

            guide me

    May the love of the Mother Earth

            nurture me

    may the True Light of my Spirit

            shine forth

in mind and soul, in heart and body

            Amen.

Born Of Woman

Everything tangible and real

      is born of Woman

           is born of the Goddess

                is born of the Feminine

      Everything

           tangible and real.

Religious, Mystical, and Occult

Most of these poems are self-explanatory. They reflect my personal outlook and experiences of a religious, mystical, or occult nature. Due to the low level of intelligence displayed by most "news" commentators it is necessary to repeatedly define occult. In contrast to the false connotations of the word, the word occult means the study of that which is unseen, a knowledge of the supernatural. An occultist is one who studies realities that are unseen, and does not have anything to do with Satanism. Satan is the devil of Christianity, a recent invention by standards of long term human history. The study of the occult is as old as humanity itself.

These poems also reflect my personal spiritual evolution. As I came to understand the strident pro-male patriarchal influences rampant in Judeo-Christian theologies, my many contentions with the Christianity of my youth and my disenchantment with the Judeo-Christian attitude towards Nature lead me to examine the beliefs of my ancestors, Cherokee, Scottish, and Irish. I decided I was philosophically more in tune with my ancestors, believing that the Earth is our sacred Mother, that Nature is divine and sacred, the physical body of the divine, and that divinity cannot be symbolized in exclusively male symbology. I did not renounce my Christian faith, rather accepted it in a pre-existing Nature religion context, as I had found on reservations and in various sweatlodges.

Plastic Jesus

You look to me like a Pharisee

    you hot-air TV preacher

and if the man came back again

    you wouldn't find his favor

you'd feel his whip upon your back

    you loud-mouthed false messiah

your money for prayers and golden temples

    were never the Master's answers.

An Apology to Jesus

    the Bride that Wasn't

I have eaten your body-bread

    I have drunk your blood as wine

My head was submerged

    My soul was cleansed

by water and by the Holy Spirit

    in body and soul was I Baptized

All done according to your scripture

    and for this I am truly grateful

but the Church I see

    cannot be your Bride

this modern day Christianity

    cannot be your Bride

or else I never knew you

    and this spiritual feeling lied

or maybe your truth is still hidden somewhere

    between the lines so simply spoken.

Maybe I don't comprehend

    because I don't like or understand

all that patriarchal bullshit

    your Semitic tribes laid down

My ancestors were Scottish, and Irish, and Cherokee

    they rode no camels, lived in no desert

and saw themselves not as the children of guilt and sin

    but as the children of Nature

saw the Earth as a loving Mother

    praised the beauty of Sun and Stars

But they were never taken captive

    back to Egypt or up to Persia

never had their asses kicked and persecuted

    for over a millennia

but for no more, for Israel stands tall and proud

    a nation filled with fighting Jews

a nation that may be around

    for eons more.

But the difference between the patriarchal Judaic/Christians

    and the matrilineal Cherokees

is not the reason

    that the Bride-that-wasn't

finds itself a stinking, rotting corpse

It is that today's scribes and Pharisees

    are worse than those

that Jesus, with bullwhip in hand,

    from his Father's house drove.

Jim Baker and Jimmy Swaggart,

    money and TV for Jesus

could not be, for Him, a Bride

    the Catholic Church, with all its Spanish-Incan blood

Nazi-Jewish blood, Pagan-Inquisition blood

    and all the stupid fucking missionaries

however well intentioned

    spreading guilt and V.D.

and measles and smallpox

    they killed off millions and millions

Where is the Love of Jesus

    in all this greed and shortsightedness

Dear Lord

    I can believe

I can believe your mother was a virgin

    made love to a god-form

had You, the precious baby

    who grew to perform

a prescribed ritual sacrifice

    so that anybody and everybody

would have somebody to believe in

    especially if they felt riddled with guilt

like the guilt used in a patriarchy

    to keep the woman-snake-lover

                            down.

Spiritual Longing

I think about the desert often

    and the Mystery it conceals

I think of friends and teachers

    how much there is to learn and share

I smell sage and the scents of the Sweatlodge

    feel the warmth of tobacco in my throat

I can hear the hissing of steam rising

    feel the relief when the drinking water comes

There is knowledge and power there

    there are people of wisdom and love

between the mountains part of my heart is captured

    because the Spirit touched me there.

Second Ring of Night

I once was told

    by an occultist wise and old

how the Word did make the world

    First was the Will, the Word, the Thought

that made the first, the very first thing

    the Ring Pass Not.

Inside the Ring, and outside too

    Lay the Constant Night, the Cosmic Womb

from which comes all life

    and inside the Ring

were all worlds made.

And as the Word created Life

    right after Love, right after Light

there had to be, to balance Life

    some force of Unlife.

This force of Unlife, once made was cast

      Out past the Ring that held in Life

out past the Second Ring of Night

      Into the Void, eternal Night

there to begin the eternal fight

      Against the Life Force.

Ode to Isis

How many nights, I can't recall

I yearn for Thee

this Mystery to solve

of which You are the Night

and long I've gazed upon the Moon

basking in Her glow and Light

and through these veils with purpose

I, one by one, have passed

and yet Thou remain enigma

unending Mystery so Vast.

A Spirit Goes Shining
A Tribute to Evelyn Eaton

One of the best people in the world has passed on

    there is little I can say

One of the finest people I ever knew has gone on

    and there is little I can do

        to help in any way

    But I can send a voice unto the heavens

        to bless her

    I send a voice unto the Good and Gentle Spirit

       to guide her and be with her

  I send a voice unto the Great, Great Spirit

        that a part is coming home

          which never left.

Fabric and Friction of Reality

The fear of non-existence

    and the will of that which exists

to continue to exist

    is the friction that provides the fabric of the Universe

It provides the duality, the polar opposites

    which live and die, and yet continue

It would be pointless if all Mysteries were solved

    God exists to exist

It would be fruitless

    if everything were already answered

There must be friction and opposition

    There must be Life.

There is a Good Side to the Darkness

There is a good side to the Darkness

    and a bad side to the Light

To harm none and do what you will

    is a harmless way of life

But I would stop the war we wage

    Man against the Earth

I have Desire but not the Knowledge

    I have no weapons, but the Will.

Eternity Waits

Eternity waits

> long moments

>> to be tapped on the shoulder

the Soul of the Universe

> deep down

>> waiting to be beholden.

Materialists Denial

When people make the spiritual connection

> and have the advent of Power

it is proof positive of the Spirit

> and the materialists denial.

Tools

Searching, seeking in the shadows

    with the tools of Dark and Light

We shall find that hidden Being

    the Light that lays beneath the Night

In the Darkness, out of Darkness

    forge we now these tools of Light

in this circle, this our world now

    we have cleared the path for Light

We invoke Thee

    O Great Vast One

        Mother of Darkness

            Father of Light

Fill our souls now

    with Thy Love-Force

Fill our spirits

    with Thy Light

Fill our bodies, hearts and minds now

    with Thy ever-healing Light.

Invocation of the Sun

I am the Light needed by the Darkness

    I am the Face of the Sun

I am He who gives Love-Light to the Moon

    I am He who seeds Life upon the Earth.

I am Helios the Sun

    I am Amen Ra rising

I am the sun-god reborn

    I am Light transforming Darkness.

Face of God

God has but one face

           Truth

Evil has a thousand faces

           and all of them are lies.

Prayer to the Gracious Goddess

Gracious Goddess, Thou Who art the Source and Beauty

I a human, do beseech Thee

that if, in my wayward moments

I momentarily forget Thee

May Thou, in thy Love

never forget me.

Ancestors

As I look into my nature and my genes

on the endless quest of self-discovery

I look to find my ancestors

and realize, despite the weight of cultural belief

my people are fifteen parts Scotts-Irish

and a sixteenth part Creek/Cherokee

My ancestors were <u>not</u> people of the Book

we're not from tribes obsessed by guilt

nor tribes obsessed with martyrdom.

The Scotts-Irish blood in me

screams for Moonlight and the heath

not dreary, dusty, desert wars

my tribes lived and died a natural life

a life of natural beauty

living sacredly on Mother Earth

worshipping inside tall rings of stone

those are my genes

and I hear the anguished screams of Cherokees

on their endless trail of tears.

I feel my blood, I feel my genes

but not dominion, sin, or guilt

not the angry needs of a righteous God

but rather Nature's Truth.

All Known

We have all known

    fear, hurt, shame, and injury

let these things of the past

    not block the energy of our own divinity

but rather may they be healed by it.

Wrestling Devils

They say I look tired

    and I feel so tired

I'm spent in body, soul, and mind.

I've wrestled with a devil

    that I had in my hold

that devil got tired of wrestling

    that devil, he let go

all along I thought he held me

    but when that devil tried to flee

I found out much to my surprise

    it was only me.

We all have our angels and demons

    we all have our darkness and light

and we must come to accept them both

    and the transcendent oneness of Life.

Womb of the Worlds

Out of the Womb of the Worlds

    came and stayed

        the first Light

    Understanding cannot come

        to the Mystery

           of How

The Darkness

    Womb of Potential Life

        Willed forth

           the Word

        the Sound

           the Light

the I Am That I Am

    which became

        and remained

           the Light

the Source and Sustenance

    are One

the Darkness knew the Light

    that they should bear children

        the children of Life.

God is a Whale

God is a Whale

    swimming through

        the Ocean of Space and Time

our minds reflect God's Mind

    as human creations

        mirror the minds' of humanity.

The Whale keeps swimming on.

Insanity, the Lure of Death, and the Dance of Life

I've been there on the edge of sanity

    balancing

        feeling the pull of the waves

I've been there

    and known the nearness of madness

knowing there was a precipe

    knowing what I was risking there

        standing too close to the edge

I've been there

    driven by the hurt and pain

        the relentless constancy of my torment

I've fearlessly walked that edge

    and felt part of myself

willing...

willing to go over

    to maybe find a certain rest

        perhaps a gentle peace

        perhaps a gentle peace

I've been there and felt the swift strong pull of the currents

    their dark and secret undertows

        pulling me out to sea oblivious

I've been there on the edge

    and felt and known there must be some escape

        some peace, some restful deep

and there may be

    but the lure of death and madness

        surely wears the face of chaos

            a face failing to seduce.

Still, I seek the Darkness with great proclivity

    it rises from my nature

it's not that I fore shun the Light

    rather I embrace it

but all of Life is made of halves

    the Darkness and the Light

the fulfillment comes when both halves join

    transcended by spirit divine

and their joining gives birth to the child within

    thus goes the dance of Life

two halves join to become something more

    and give birth to the being of Light

and all of Life does do this dance

    the Darkness and the Light

the clothing worn by God above

    gives being to the Child

the Child is all that lives and breathes

    the matter and stuff of Life

and all that is, is born of Mother

    and Fathered by the Light.

Alice Named Isis

Alice named Isis

    the looking glass mirror

        of the mind

Run along and find yourself

    running there inside

catch me   catch you

    catch up

  with myself

Alice named Isis

  explore the mirror

    for yourself.

God the Goddess - Out of Reach

God is a cloud

  of Oneness

Always approaching

  but always changing

    somehow slightly out of reach

but God the Goddess is a Gracious Goddess

    who loves her children

        loves us each

but God the Goddess is duality

    that's always calling and approaching

        but is always

            ever gently out of reach

because if we had it all

    what would be the purpose

        God the Goddess

            stays out of reach.

Don't Be Waylaid

Don't get waylaid

    by your lower emotions

don't be a slave

    to lust and greed

give to your life

    your <u>own</u> direction

follow the path

    where your true heart leads.

Excuses

Tell it to the poor and sick

    tell it to the lame

tell it to the Star Child

    who was tempted but refrained

Tell it to the empty dark

    or to the empty glass

I don't care about excuses

    tell it to the rest.

The Universe

The Universe

    is experienced

through our perceptions

    of it.

God sees and beholds

    the magnificence

        of Its Oneness

through the myriad perceptions

    that perceive it.

The Duality

    is That Which Perceives

        and That Which Is Perceived

and that which flows between

    Balancing

        And Transcending Both.

For God

the loneliness

    I seek a solution to

is not the loneliness

    of a man for a woman

but of a human for God.

Need for Forgiveness

Maybe there's something about going to the love of Jesus

    for forgiveness

        one too many times

            that makes it seem so insincere

Maybe this need for forgiveness

    should be forgiven

I'm a child of God, a child of Earth

    a child of woman, a child of man

I'm a child of Mother Earth and Father Sun

    doing the Dance of Love

in my parents' bedroom

    I'm a child of Love

I guess when it gets down to it

    I'm a child of love

and so, I guess, was Jesus - as are we all.

Yahweh's Consort

They've found 4000 statues of Asherah

    near the Old Temple in Jerusalem

the Lion-Lady was kept out of the Temple

    they shunned the consort of their maker

the Temple priests distrusted women

God the God made in male image

so Asherah was kept outside

    living in the hearts of women.

No Longer on Bended Knee

I come to Thee

    no longer

    on bended knee

    but eye to eye

    with dignity

For am I not of Thee?

Is that Divinity

    which Thou art

    not also

    within me?

Am I not Thine already?

Religion/Liberation - Real Religious Experience

a <u>real</u>

    religious experience

        liberates

            the experiencer

a valid and true

    religious experience

        is not taught or learned

    but experienced

Religion equals Liberation

    in that

<u>true</u> religious experience = spiritual liberation.

The Miracle of Unanswered Prayer

How many times

      have you prayed for something

something you really wanted

      at that point in your life

and you didn't get it

      and temporarily

you were angry

      or unhappy

But then as you grew

      and time went on

you were more than thankful

      that what you prayed for

did not come about

We have human limitations of perception.

Sometimes, the perfect answer

            to prayer

                is no.

Catastrophe and the Search for Meaning

Too many people

    just go through life

        they don't fully explore life

            or search for its meaning

Too many people

    wait for catastrophe to strike

        before they ever think

            to search for meaning

But once catastrophe

    rocks their boat

        they begin to search

            to seek Life's meaning

for Life does have meaning

    Purpose

        and Spiritual Reward

for those who pierce the veilings.

That Sacred Somehow-Other

every man

    every woman

        every child

    is always alone

is never alone

    because that infinite part

does dwell within

    that sacred somehow-other

we always seek

    but only find inside

and reunited

    the "I" self

the shadow-self

    and the light-self

transcend

        to

            god-self.

Iki-ryo

The Japanese call it

    the iki-ryo

we call it the demon

    or the devil inside

but we've all got a

                Guardian Angel

always standing there

                beside

maybe the stronger the

                Angel

the stronger the demon

                inside

that might help to explain so much

    of the contradictions

                and paradoxes

                    of Life.

Maybe it's part of the

                    battle

the yin and the yang there

                    inside

but there's always

                    the Chi

that transcends them

                    both

the Breath

            of the God-Force

                    of Life.

My Revelation

My revelation

        is not a new Goddess

                or God

but that all Goddesses are

one Goddess

All that is, is the marriage of

    the God and Goddess

and the Divine Spirit Which Transcends.

However the Beauty of Life

    calls to you to be worshipped

        that is good.

If I have a revelation

    it is as old as this planet

        and as new as the next moment

It is that Gaia lives

    this planet is alive

        She is our Mother.

www.ingramcontent.com/pod-product-compliance
Lightning Source LLC
Chambersburg PA
CBHW080554090426
42735CB00016B/3236